Table of Contents

The Third Rock from

Whether we see them or not, rocks are constantly under our feet, or sometimes rising far above us as mountains. They are products of a much bigger rock, this Third Rock from the Sun we call Earth. That's why understanding rocks, **minerals**, **geodes**, and gems helps us understand the world in which we live.

We live on Earth's crust, the thinnest layer, which is made largely of the **igneous** rock granite. (More about igneous rock on p. 16.) Just beneath that is the much-thicker upper mantle, made of solid rock closer to the surface and **molten** rock farther down.

Then comes the lower mantle—which stays solid, despite the heat, because of pressure. At the very center of our planet are the metallic outer core and molten inner core, with temperatures hundreds to thousands of times hotter than on the surface.

INNER CORE

CORE

MANTLE

CRUST

Rock-Hard Fact

Earth is a giant ball of rock weighing about 6 sextillion—that's 6 followed by 21 zeros!—tons (5.4 sextillion tonnes). Our planet's rock layers go hundreds of miles deep.

6,000,000,000,000,000,000,000

the Sun

Scientists believe Earth's surface is made up
of floating plates of rock. These plates
always move a little—so little we can't feel it.
But when they move a lot, they collide
and cause **volcanoes** or earthquakes.
Our planet has about 1,500 active
volcanoes, many under the sea, with
between 50 and 60 eruptions a
year. Every day, hundreds of minor
earthquakes take place, with at
least one major one somewhere
in the world each month.

It all starts with minerals

The atomic number for gold is 79.

79
Au
Gold 196.96

Minerals are the building blocks of rocks and gems. They're made of **atoms** arranged in a **uniform** pattern. Just like humans, who have one-of-kind DNA and fingerprints, minerals have certain properties that make them unique. Their properties result from their **composition** and how their atoms are arranged.

Quartz

Calcite

Graphite

Magnetite

Gold

Talc	Gypsum	Calcite
1	2	3

S O F T

6 properties of minerals

Minerals have special features called properties that make them different from one another. Let's look at six of them.

1. Specific gravity: How heavy is it compared with the same amount of water?

2. Luster: Is it shiny or dull?

shiny

dull

Pyrite

Cinnabar

3. Transparency: Can you shine a flashlight through it?

4. Hardness: Is it soft enough to scratch with a fingernail or another rock, or does it leave a scratch mark behind instead?

5. Color: What color is it?

Fuchsite   Corundum

6. Streak: When you rub it across a rough surface, what color streak does it make? The streak test shows the mineral's true color. For instance, the mineral hematite can appear black, white, red, or silver. But you can identify it by its red streak.

Mohs Scale of Hardness
Minerals are assigned numbers according to their hardness.

Fluorite	Apatite	Orthoclase	Quartz		Topaz	Corundum	Diamond

4	5	6	7		8	9	10

M E D I U M   **H A R D**

Dare to Compare

Geologists and **mineralogists** learn about rocks and minerals by studying them. Let's put your rocks to the test and see what you can learn about them.

1. Magnetism: Is your rock drawn to a magnet? If so, your rock contains the mineral iron.

2. Floating: Drop your rock into a plastic cup filled with water. If your rock floats, you have a **porous** igneous rock known as pumice.

3. Hardness: Try to scratch your rock with your fingernail. Then scratch your rocks against one another. Whichever one is most easily scratched is the softest according to the Mohs scale. The one that leaves the most scratch marks is the hardest.

4. Streak Test: With an adult's help, find a single white tile, or use the bottom of a white ceramic coffee mug. Rub your rock on the dull, or unglazed, side of it. Does the streak color match the rock color, or is it different? The streak shows you the rock's true color.

5. Luster: Wash your rocks with warm water, and let them air dry. Is one or more of them shiny? If so, it has luster. A rock with luster sometimes contains a type of metal.

6. Transparency: Hold a flashlight behind each rock. If the light shines through it, your rock is transparent. If it doesn't, your rock is **opaque**.

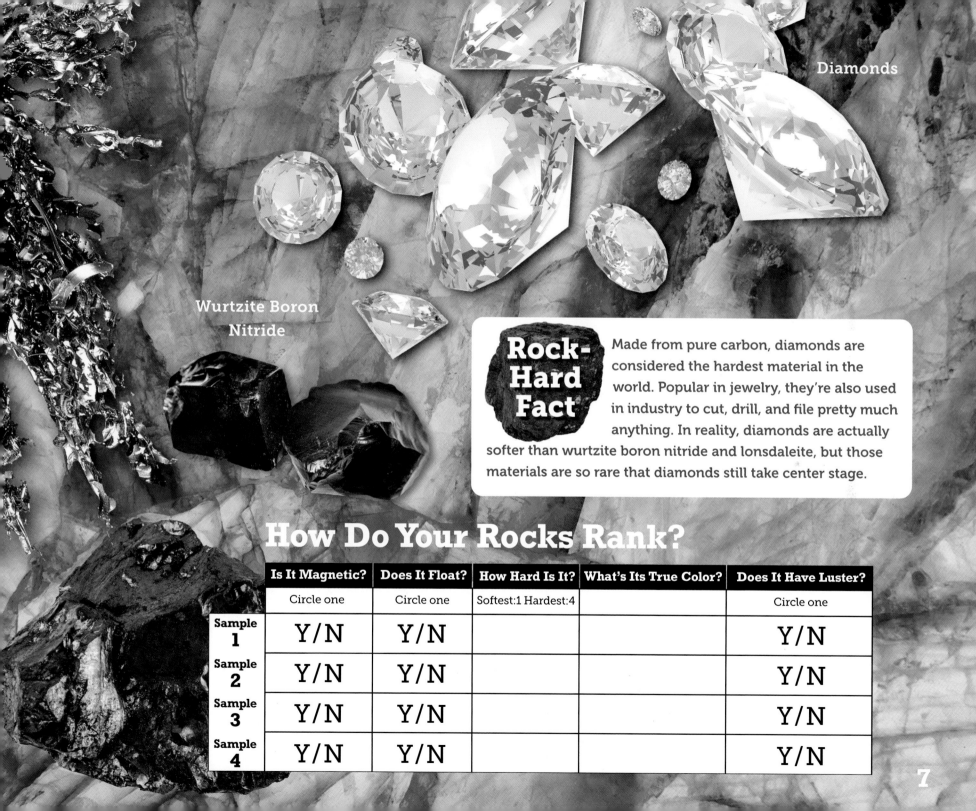

Diamonds

Wurtzite Boron Nitride

Rock-Hard Fact

Made from pure carbon, diamonds are considered the hardest material in the world. Popular in jewelry, they're also used in industry to cut, drill, and file pretty much anything. In reality, diamonds are actually softer than wurtzite boron nitride and lonsdaleite, but those materials are so rare that diamonds still take center stage.

How Do Your Rocks Rank?

	Is It Magnetic?	Does It Float?	How Hard Is It?	What's Its True Color?	Does It Have Luster?
	Circle one	Circle one	Softest:1 Hardest:4		Circle one
Sample 1	Y/N	Y/N			Y/N
Sample 2	Y/N	Y/N			Y/N
Sample 3	Y/N	Y/N			Y/N
Sample 4	Y/N	Y/N			Y/N

Strange-But-True Stories:

Mind-Blowing Mercury

The Mad Hatter of *Alice in Wonderland* is based on history, and you can blame mercury for his strange behavior. Mercury, a mineral and **element** usually found in liquid form, is used in thermometers and science. It was used as medicine—until it was found to be **toxic**.

In the 1800s, mercury was used to improve the felt used in hat making. Before mercury, hatmakers used urine! The problem was, mercury made hatmakers drool, talk to themselves, and shake, prompting the term "mad as a hatter."

Color-Changing Minerals

Some minerals may change color under ultraviolet light. Autunite changes from a yellowish color to a spooky green. Even spookier, it glows because it's **radioactive**! It contains the element uranium, used in making bombs and generating power.

This glowing effect is called **fluorescence**, a term named after the mineral fluorite. Fluorite may be the most colorful mineral of them all. It can even change color under sunlight or appear to have bands of color.

Other minerals—like amazonite and labradorite—seem to change colors when viewed from different angles. This changing ability is known as **iridescence**.

Labradorite

Amazonite

Rock-Hard Fact

Strange as it sounds, recycling electronic devices can protect gorillas, chimpanzees, and elephants. When the metallic mineral coltan—used in electronics—is harvested in parts of Africa, it can destroy habitat for these animals. If coltan is recycled, less needs to be mined, resulting in less destruction of habitats.

Coltan

Magnetite

Do you ever wonder how animals have such a good sense of direction, giving them the ability to travel hundreds or even thousands of miles to specific locations? They can thank the mineral magnetite, which is found in their brains. It gives them an ability known as magnetoreception so they can create mental maps to their destinations.

Common Minerals

Minerals are always solid. When a mineral turns liquid from heat, it stops being a mineral. Minerals result when **magma** melts and cools beneath the earth's surface. Water evaporates, leaving behind minerals in crystal form. Let's get to know some of the most common minerals.

◄ Feldspar

More feldspar is found in the earth's crust than any other mineral. Most of the rocks found in the crust—rocks like granite and basalt—contain feldspar. It is found in every category of rock, including in gemstones.

Quartz ►

Quartz is another key ingredient in the earth's crust, and it may be the most useful mineral of all. It's used widely in watches and electronics because it can release an electrical charge and act as a battery of sorts. Some gemstones, such as amethyst and citrine, are made of quartz.

Citrine

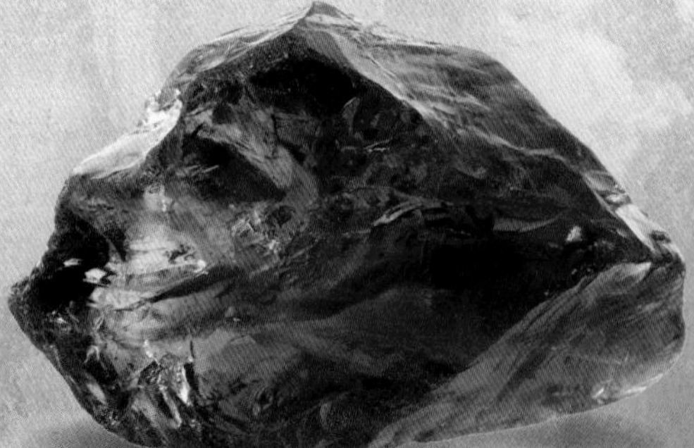

Amethyst

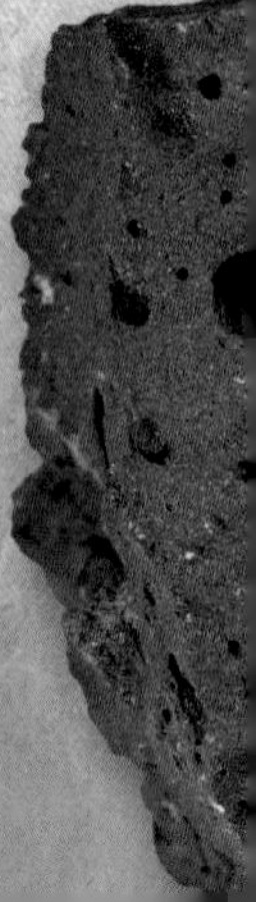

▲ Mica

Found in lesser amounts in the crust, mica forms in flat sheets. It scores a mere 2.5 on Mohs scale, so you can scratch it with your fingernail. If you ever visit Mount Rushmore National Memorial in South Dakota, you'll get a firsthand look at rocks containing mica.

▼ Olivine

Scientists believe a type of olivine, known as bridgmanite, makes up more than a third of Earth's entire volume. They believe this from studying meteorites, which form under amounts of pressure and heat similar to what is found in our planet's mantle.

Rock-Hard Fact

About a third of the water we drink comes from rocks underground. Minerals from rocks strengthen our bodies and help water taste better.

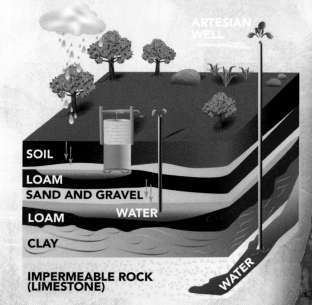

ARTESIAN WELL

SOIL
LOAM
SAND AND GRAVEL
WATER
LOAM
CLAY
IMPERMEABLE ROCK (LIMESTONE)
WATER

Minerals are found in many things other than rocks. They're also found in food. Beef, for instance, contains the mineral iron. Bananas are a good source of potassium, and dairy is a good source of calcium. These minerals, along with others, help our bodies grow and stay healthy.

Strange-But-True-Stories:
Can Minerals Zap Pollution?

In the 1940s, geologists unearthed minerals from a Siberian mine. For a long time, scientists lacked the tools to test them properly. But finally in 2010, a **chemistry** professor read an article from an old magazine about the minerals.

The professor noticed the Siberian minerals sounded a lot like man-made materials that had only been made in laboratories. No one had believed anything like these materials could ever be found in nature.

Scientists believe the minerals, now named stepanovite and zhemchuzhnikovite, can work like sponges that can soak up carbon gases in our air. A discovery like that could greatly improve our air quality and protect our environment. Scientists also think the minerals could be used to create energy. They hope to find other natural sources of the minerals and test their **theories**.

Zhemchuzhnikovite

Changing Earth's Layers

Geologists learn a lot about Earth's history by studying its **strata**. The layers tell stories of earthquakes and volcanoes, ancient animals and plants, the people who once lived here, and even the **climate**. Scientists try to figure out when events happened or when things or people lived.

But some scientists fear the strata from modern times will send a confusing message to future geologists. Building materials today can come from all over the earth. Once they break down, they will create a mash of minerals not typically found in that part of the world.

Imagine, for instance, the Washington Monument as a column of limestone within the earth where no other limestone can be found. Add to that a number of man-made minerals, and future layers could become even more confusing.

Rock-Hard Fact

Most mineral crystals are so tiny that you can only see them under a microscope. But some are larger than life! Cave of the Crystals in Chihuahua, Mexico, is home to record-breaking quartz columns measuring 36 ft. (11 m) long, 4 ft. (1.2 m) wide, and weighing about 55 tons (50 tonnes) each.

Scientists were stumped by rocks and boulders made of the mineral dolomite that seemed to propel themselves across Racetrack Playa in Death Valley National Park. In 2014, they used cameras to solve the mystery. The playa—covered in 3 in. (7 cm) of water—would freeze overnight. As the sun rose, the cracking ice and wind sent the rocks sailing.

Rock Your World

DEPOSITION

We know living things start out one way and become another. Seeds become seedlings. Seedlings become plants or trees. Babies grow into children, and children become adults. So it is with rocks. They may begin one way, but they change over time. And the change never stops.

Rocks belong to three basic groups: igneous, **metamorphic**, and **sedimentary**. Sometimes sedimentary rocks get mashed together to become **conglomerate** rocks. Heat and pressure can change one type of rock to another, and sometimes back again. **Erosion** can break down rock and cause the cycle to start all over again.

Igneous rock can get pushed to the surface, where it is worn down and turned into sedimentary rock. But then heat and pressure can turn sedimentary rock into a metamorphic rock, only to get pushed to the surface and turned back into sedimentary rock again. Or it can get pushed deeper into the earth, where it will become magma and eventually become igneous again.

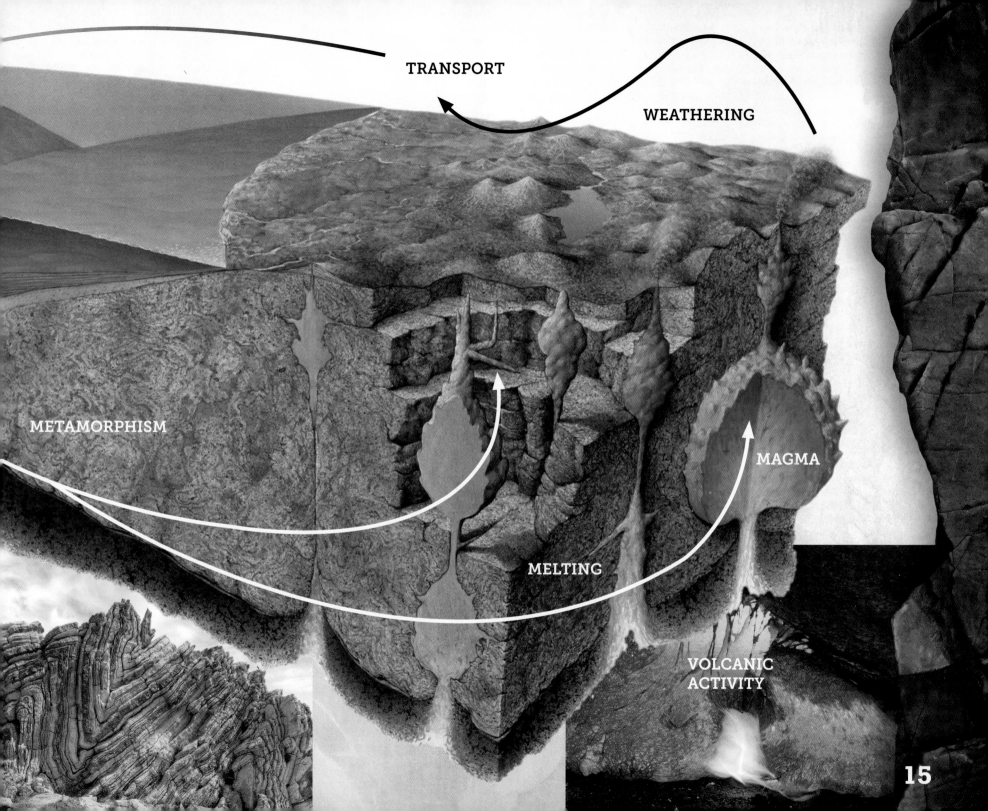

TRANSPORT

WEATHERING

METAMORPHISM

MAGMA

MELTING

VOLCANIC ACTIVITY

15

Igneous Rocks

Igneous rocks form inside the earth or on the surface when molten rock becomes solid. Underground, molten material cools slowly and creates **intrusive** rocks. But sometimes magma escapes through surface cracks or through volcanoes. This results in **extrusive** rocks.

Though sedimentary rocks are found more often on the surface, igneous rocks are actually the most common type of rock. Igneous rocks—with more than 700 different types—make up most of the earth's upper crust.

Extrusive Igneous Rock
(Magma comes out as lava and cools on the surface)

Intrusive Igneous Rock
(Magma cools off beneath the surface)

Intrusive Rocks

Gabbro

Diorite

Granite

Pegmatite

Peridotite

Dunite

Extrusive Rocks

Obsidian

Rhyolite

Andesite

Basalt

Pumice

17

Sedimentary Rocks

Sedimentary rocks are easy to spot: Just look for the layers. Like pages in a book, these layers tell a story about the rock's formation. First, erosion breaks down rocks into sediment, which becomes sand like you see on the beach or in mud.

Grains of beach sand

Layers of sediment build up, often trapping living things—plants, trees, or animals—within the layers. Sedimentary rocks that contain living things are **organic**, and rocks that don't contain living things are **inorganic**.

When living things are trapped within sedimentary rock layers, they leave an imprint, much like when you leave a footprint in sand or soft ground. We call these imprints **fossils**. Fossils are windows into a world that was, allowing us to understand ancient plant and animal life, behaviors, and climate.

Compressed layers of sediment

Fossiled footprints

Organic Sedimentary Rocks

Limestone

Oil shale

Coquina limestone

Coal

Inorganic Sedimentary Rocks

Siltstone

Gypsum

Chert

Flint

Metamorphic Rocks

When something morphs, it changes—kind of like how a fictional robot morphs into a vehicle. Metamorphic rocks don't become robots or vehicles, but they change in really amazing ways as the result of heat, pressure, and **chemical** changes.

These changes often take place deep underground, where magma produces heat and Earth's plates crash together. Earthquakes and erosion can help metamorphic rocks find their way to the surface, often around mountains. You can spot them by the twists, swirls, and folds within them.

Because the rock cycle never ends, metamorphic rocks can begin as igneous or sedimentary rocks. They can break down into sedimentary rocks and eventually become metamorphic all over again.

Phyllite

Slate

Granulite

Anthracite

Schist

Gneiss

Red marble

Quartzite

Conglomerate Rocks

Conglomerate rocks are like the blended families of the rock world. They are a special type of sedimentary rock that can contain rounded pieces of sedimentary, igneous, or metamorphic rock held together by sand or mud.

Rocks are carried along by a strong current—perhaps a river or stream—and deposited on a beach or shore. The rocks get broken down, and pieces get pushed together over time. Then sand or mud fills in gaps between them, eventually forming conglomerate rocks.

Because they're held together by sand or mud, these rocks can be easily broken. That means they can easily reform all over again. Geologists can study conglomerate rocks found in an area to determine if valuable minerals such as gold or diamonds, which may be found within them, could be nearby.

Meet an Imposter

At first glance, breccia looks like a conglomerate rock. It does, after all, contain pieces of rock held together by a type of natural cement. But there's a small difference: The pieces within breccia are angular, while the pieces within conglomerate are round. Weather changes produce the angular rock pieces over time.

A Clue to the History of Mars

A NASA rover found evidence that water was once found on the surface of Mars. The evidence: a bed of conglomerate rocks that only could have been moved by water. Scientists believe where there is water, there may be life.

Puddingstones are conglomerate rocks with dark pebbles held together by a lighter sand or mud.

Breccia

Puddingstone

Strange-But-True-Stories:

The World's Weirdest Rock Formations

Sometimes limestone beneath the surface gives way, creating sinkholes. Sinkholes on the surface are bad. Houses, cars, and even people can get sucked inside.

But sinkholes in the ocean can be beautiful, as proven by the Blue Hole off the coast of Belize. The massive sinkhole measures 984 ft. (276.5 m) across and 407 ft. (124 m) deep. Divers explore it to see the marine life within it.

Blue Hole in Belize

Antelope Canyon in Arizona

The Original State of the Sunshine State

Most of us can easily find Florida on a map. It's that long fingerlike state—the one with all the sunshine, water, and great vacation spots. But long ago, finding Florida might not have been as easy as heading south from Georgia.

In fact, Florida might not have been in what became the United States, or even in North America. Scientists say the rocks beneath Florida show it originally was part of Africa or South America. They believe two plates beneath the surface crashed together, causing Florida to break off and attach itself to North America. Will the Sunshine State stay put? Only time will tell.

Rock-Hard Fact

For thousands of years, massive columns of stone—most upright, with others laid across the tops of them—have mystified scientists. Some of the stones weigh 4.4 tons (4 tonnes) each. How did they get there? What was their purpose? The site, known as Stonehenge, is a popular tourist destination in Great Britain and still remains a mystery.

In the 1970s, a man named Gary Dahl made $15 million selling a new type of pet that came in a cardboard box with a bed of straw inside. This pet didn't eat, poop, play, or require attention of any kind. So what was this miracle pet? It was a pet rock. Dahl priced his pet rocks at $3.95 each, selling 1 million in 1975 alone.

Start Your Own Rock Collection

Starting your own rock collection is fun and easy. Here are a few tips for getting started:

Identify sources. With an adult's help, research what types of rocks can be found in your area. Do you live near mountains, a river or stream, a lake, or an ocean? All of those areas will offer a wealth of rock samples.

Get a few basic tools. You'll need a backpack, work gloves, goggles, a rock hammer, a rock chisel, a magnifying glass, a camera or camera phone, and sturdy shoes. Also remember to pack plenty of water and snacks!

Be observant and take notes. Take pictures of each sample as you find it. Assign it a number, and write down what you observe about it and where you found it.

Clean rocks carefully. Wash them in warm water and mild soap. Use a soft brush to scrub off excess dirt. Let them air-dry.

Store and label your samples. Store each rock separately in an egg carton, and identify it by its type, if you can identify it, or its number using sticky labels.

Study your rocks. Note how they compare in hardness. What can you observe about their properties? (See pp. 6-7.)

Find a local geology or mineralogy club. There's strength in numbers! Ask an adult to help you find a club so you can learn more about collecting and identifying rocks.

Ask a professional for help. If identifying a particular rock proves tricky, ask for help from a geologist with a state university or natural history museum.

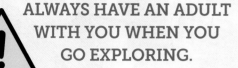

ALWAYS HAVE AN ADULT
WITH YOU WHEN YOU
GO EXPLORING.
Ask for the adult's help
when you use tools, and
wear goggles when you use
a hammer or chisel.

Make Them Shine!

Bring out the beauty of your rocks by
dabbing petroleum jelly onto a cotton
cloth or old towel and rubbing it evenly
over the entire surface of the rock.

Rock-Hard Fact

Many places around the
world, including most US
states, have dig sites. You
can bring your family and
your rock collecting gear,
and take home rock
samples for a small fee.

Do-It-Yourself Rock Weathering

Have you ever seen an old barn that's barely standing? It shows the effects of years of exposure to the rain, wind, and sun. Even though rocks are much harder than the wood in old barns, they also experience the effects of **weathering**.

Biological Weathering

You've probably seen a plant or tree root that breaks through a sidewalk. This is an example of **biological** weathering. Tree roots can crack rocks, and slow-growing plants such as lichen can break down rocks and even change their composition.

Chemical Weathering

Rocks also undergo change through chemical weathering. Water, acids, and gases slowly dissolve or react with minerals in the rock, creating new compounds. Would you like to try to recreate this process? Take a look at the instructions on the next page.

Let's apply lemon juice and vinegar—weak acids found in most kitchens—to two of your rocks. What do you think will happen?

⚠ **GET YOUR PARENT'S PERMISSION BEFORE STARTING THIS PROJECT!**

What You Do

1. Put a few drops of lemon juice on one rock.
2. Put a few drops of vinegar on the second rock.
3. Listen carefully!

What Happens Next?

Did you hear a fizzing sound? Lemon juice and vinegar contain acetic acid, which dissolves calcium carbonate. Acetic acid will cause limestone, chalk, or calcite to fizz. But quartz, which doesn't contain calcium carbonate, will not react to acetic acid.

Strange-But-True-Stories:

Menacing Meteorites!

Vredefort Crater in South Africa

Most meteors burn up as they enter Earth's atmosphere. Despite that, about 500 meteorites hit Earth's surface each year. These impacts can be deadly, killing everything and everyone around them. Some scientists believe a meteorite impact caused dinosaurs to become extinct.

The biggest impact crater, Vredefort Crater in South Africa, measures about 236 mi. (380 km) in diameter. It is so large that it can only be seen in full from space.

Scientists say a house-sized meteorite could flatten buildings for miles around. But even smaller ones can shatter windows as they enter our atmosphere or cause sunburns from the light energy they release.

Lifeless surface of Mars

Moon Rocks! Mars Rocks!

Astronauts from NASA's Apollo Moon missions brought back more than 800 lbs. (363 kg) of **lunar** rock for scientists to study. Interestingly, the samples were common to our planet—rocks like basalt, anorthosite, and breccia. But unlike their earthly counterparts, lunar rocks are worth millions of dollars each.

Scientists are also studying the rocks on Mars using NASA's unmanned rovers. Some of Mars's surface looks much like the sandstone found in the Southwestern United States. Other areas are covered in sedimentary mudstone, hinting at an ancient bed of water.

Rock-Hard Fact

Moon rock

Impact craters on Earth's surface get weathered or eroded over time. But craters on the moon look just like they did the day they happened. That's because the moon doesn't have weather, water, and plants like the earth does.

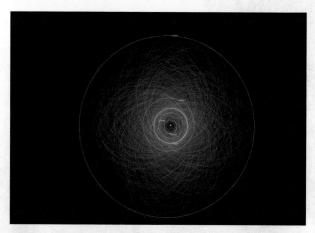

Chances are you've never seen a map like this one. This is a map of what the space agency NASA calls "potentially hazardous asteroids"—more than 1,400 of them. "These are the asteroids considered hazardous because they are fairly large (at least 460 ft. or 140 m in size), and because they follow orbits that pass close to the earth's orbit (within 4.7 million mi. or 7.5 million km)," NASA officials wrote. But don't be too worried. None of the asteroids is expected to hit in the next 100 years.

Glorious Gems

Gems are like the royalty of the mineral world: They're valued for their rarity. The rarer a gem, the more valuable it is. When they're rough—meaning uncut and unpolished—they may look like pretty rocks, but an expert can bring out their color and fire. Fire describes the way gems seem to flash different colors of light, as if each stone contains a rainbow within itself.

WHAT IS YOUR BIRTHSTONE?

Birthstones are gemstones that are assigned to birth months. Can you spot your birthstone?

JANUARY GARNET	FEBRUARY AMETHYST	MARCH AQUAMARINE
APRIL DIAMOND	MAY EMERALD	JUNE PEARL
JULY RUBY	AUGUST PERIDOT	SEPTEMBER SAPPHIRE
OCTOBER TOURMALINE	NOVEMBER CITRINE	DECEMBER BLUE TOPAZ

Turquoise

Amethyst

Topaz

Garnet

Citrine

Sapphire

Rough ruby

Rose quartz

Opal

Aquamarine

Diamond

Raw emerald

Scientists have found a way to make gems more affordable by creating them in a laboratory. Lab-created gems have the exact same composition as the ones found in nature. But unlike natural stones, they contain fewer flaws. And because no mining is required, they're also easier on the environment and safer to produce.

33

The Stars That Shine Brightest

More than 4,000 minerals are found on Earth. Of those, fewer than 100 are worthy to be called gems. And of those, an even smaller number can claim star status. Let's meet a few of them.

The Hope Diamond

At 45.42 carats, it's hard to place a value on this beautiful blue diamond, which is said to be cursed. Beheadings, murders, and accidents have befallen its many owners. But were the stories made up just to increase the rare diamond's value?

The Black Prince's Ruby

The story of this stone—which is not actually a ruby but is an uncut spinel—begins in the 15th century, when Don Pedro the Cruel murdered its owner, the Moorish Prince of Granada. Pedro took the chicken egg-sized stone but made a deal to give it to Prince Edward III of England. It is on display with the British crown jewels.

The Andamooka Opal

The South Australian government gave this 203-carat opal, considered the finest opal ever found because of its rich colors, to Queen Elizabeth of England in 1954. But the queen doesn't seem to be much of an opal fan and has kept the opal necklace in a vault after wearing it briefly.

The Star of India

The size of a golf ball, this 563-carat gem is the world's largest star sapphire. The mineral rutile gives the world-famous gem its milky color and produces a star pattern when light is reflected on the stone. Stolen from the American Museum of Natural History in New York City in 1964, it has been back on display since being found two days later.

Rock-Hard Fact

Cutting and polishing a gem brings out its inner beauty, but it comes at a cost. A gem can lose as much as **70 percent** of its weight in the process.

Gemstones That Command Respect

These gems rank among the most expensive in the world.

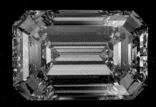

Blue diamond
Up to $3.93 million per carat

Red diamond
$1 million per carat

Musgravite
$35,000 per carat

Alexandrite
$12,000 per carat

Crystal Systems

If you like minerals and gems, prepare to like geometry! The crystals in minerals and gems are made of six geometric shapes.

CUBIC
Example: Halite

TETRAGONAL
Example: Zircon

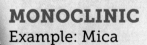

HEXAGONAL
Example: Quartz

ORTHORHOMBIC
Example: Staurolite

MONOCLINIC
Example: Mica

TRICLINIC
Example: Rhodonite

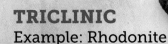

Strange-But-True Stories:
Suffering Sapphires!

Today people value sapphires for their beautiful blue color. But in ancient times, they were valued for their supposed health benefits.

People would grind sapphires into powder. Then they ate it. They believed ground sapphires would cure aches and pains, stomach issues in babies, and mental illness. They also believed it would improve eyesight.

Sapphires were assigned other powers as well. They were believed to kill snakes and prevent people from being jealous about other people's property or luck. Today their power is over pocketbooks, with sapphires selling for as much as $11,000 per carat.

Amber

Rock-Hard Fact

Pearls, coral, and amber are organic gems. Pearls are the only gems created by living animals. Coral actually is the skeleton of a living animal. Amber, made from tree **resin**, comes from a living thing.

Gems with Alien Origins

We've talked about how horrible things like death and destruction can result when meteorites hit Earth. But so can beautiful things, such as the gem-quality glasses known as moldavite and Libyan Desert glass, or the gem pallasite.

Moldavite resulted from what scientists think was a meteorite impact long, long ago in what is now Germany. The meteorite broke into two pieces and hit with enough heat and force to melt surrounding rock. Libyan Desert glass formed in the same way in Africa long ago.

But pallasite is otherworldly. It comes from an actual meteorite and is highly valued as a gem. Is it by chance pallasite is an alien green? You decide.

Rock-Hard Fact

Impurities are elements found in small amounts in gems. They are what gives gems their colors. Chromium makes a ruby appear red, while iron makes a topaz appear honey-colored.

Moldavite

Libyan Desert glass

Pallasite

Everyday Gems

Gemstones aren't just beautiful. They're useful. And whether you know it or not, you probably use them every day. Quartz, for instance, is commonly used in making glass and mining natural gas. The mineral and gem is also used in clocks, watches, and electronics. Quartz clocks and watches are more accurate than other timepieces, and quartz crystals can be found in cell phones, computers, games, and other electronics.

As for diamonds, the most treasured of all gems, only about three of every ten diamonds found is gem quality. Most diamonds are too flawed, oddly shaped, small, or poorly colored to be used as jewels. But their hardness and crystal structure ensure none will go to waste.

Because they can cut through anything, diamonds are used in drill bits and saw blades. The structure of diamonds also helps improve sound quality in speakers. Because diamonds are heat- and abrasion-resistant, they are used to make windows for X-ray machines, lasers, and vacuum chambers. They are also useful in electronics as well as in polishing and grinding.

Ranking a 9 of 10 on the Mohs scale, sapphires are hard enough to be useful in industry, especially in electronics. Scientists have been making sapphire glass using a compound found in the gem since 1902. Sapphire glass is used in electronics such as smartphones and watches, in barcode scanners at grocery stores, and also in the windows of military vehicles. The extra-strong lab-made glass is tough enough to be used as armor to protect troops in battle.

Rock-Hard Fact

In 1969, a ruby-powered laser beam 100,000 times as bright as the sun was successfully bounced off the moon. The laser helped scientists understand more about the moon, and it will help them understand more about other moons and planets. Modern lasers use different minerals to produce different types of laser beams.

39

The Hidden Beauty of Geodes

Have you ever opened a plain box and discovered something wonderful inside? Geodes are like the plain boxes of the rock world. On the outside, they don't look like anything special. That's because they hide their beauty inside.

Geodes form in igneous rock, where crystals grow from minerals within the rock in voids created by gas bubbles. They can also form in sedimentary rock, where minerals fill cavities with the help of time, pressure, space, and heat.

Calcite crystals and quartz often line the insides of geodes. But that's not all. Purple amethyst crystals can fill the rock. Some of the more valuable geodes contain opal or gem silica.

GEM SILICA GEODE

Geode
cavity

no cavity
Thunder Egg

Thunder eggs—the state rock of Oregon—are first cousins to geodes. From the outside, they look the same. Inside, they look almost the same. Both are filled with beautiful crystals and gems. However, geodes have a **cavity**, and thunder eggs do not.

Many geodes are small enough to fit in your hand, but this one can contain you. Crystal Cave in Put-in-Bay, Ohio, is the world's largest geode. Workers discovered the cave in 1897 while digging a well. Many of the blue crystals were harvested to use in fireworks before the cave became a tourist attraction.

41

Strange-But-True Stories:

Now That's a Rock!

If you saw someone wearing a 1-carat amethyst ring, you might say, "What a rock!" That's how people sometimes describe large gemstones in jewelry. But the Empress of Uruguay, the world's largest amethyst geode, is large enough to make all other big amethysts jealous.

Standing 11 ft. (3.4 m) tall and weighing 2.5 tons (2.3 tonnes), the giant geode is filled with sparkling,gem-quality amethysts. It was found in a part of Uruguay where many amethysts are found through mining, but no one had ever found anything quite like this.

The founders of Australia's Crystal Caves Museum bought the geode for $75,000 in 2007, and then they spent another $25,000 to ship it 9,100 mi. (14,645 km) to the museum in Queensland, Australia. Once there, it took two large cranes to lift the geode into place.

Cracking the Case of Crystallized Croc Eggs

Geologists don't often find prehistoric crocodile eggs because the shells were too thin for the eggs to fossilize. Instead, the eggs would just break down into the ground.

But in 1930, a fossil hunter came across some unusual geodes in Wyoming. More than 60 years later, scientists studied the quartz- and calcite-filled geodes and determined they are ancient crocodile eggs. Like other geodes, they began with an empty space inside that grew crystals with the help of time, pressure, space, and heat.

"After burial, the interior of each egg **decomposed**, and the resulting void was filled in by calcite and quartz crystals, creating a geode-like structure," a **paleontologist** explained.

Courtesy of A. Telfer/Smithsonian Institution

Rock-Hard Fact

There are stories of people finding objects other than crystals inside geodes. Some claim to have found anything from frogs to spark plugs. However, there hasn't been any confirmation about whether these were actually geodes or naturally occurring buildup of sediment around the objects.

Do you want to take a crack at discovering your own geode? Many states have geode dig sites open to the public. Among them are the Dugway Geode Beds in Utah, Geode State Park in Iowa, Rockhound State Park in New Mexico, and Jacob's Geode Mine in Illinois. Bring your own rock collecting gear, water, and snacks, along with money for park admission.

43

So You Want to be a Rock Star

Rocks, minerals, gems, and geodes have many stories to tell if we study them carefully. In fact, some scientists spend their entire lives unearthing the history, beauty, and power found within them. What kind of rock star do you want to grow up to be?

Gemologist

Gemologists are experts in gems. They can identify types of gemstones and determine their quality and value. They often study gems using magnifying glasses or microscopes.

Geologist

Geologists study materials within the earth and the history they reveal. They also study events such as landslides, volcanoes, floods, and earthquakes.

Mineralogist

Mineralogists study the chemical and crystal structures of minerals. Sometimes they work for mining companies so they can collect, prepare, and test samples.

Gemologist

Geologist

Mineralogist

Crystallographer

If you have an eye for detail and you love science, crystallography could be in your future. **Crystallographers** study crystals— such as those found in minerals— at the atomic level, and they have to be experts in many areas of science. They study everything from gemstones to viruses.

Crystallographer

Archeologist

Archeologists dig human history—literally! They search for **artifacts** and remains that give clues about the people who once lived in a certain area. By studying what they find, they can learn about how the people lived, what they wore, what they ate, and what was important to them.

Archeologist

Glossary

ARCHEOLOGIST
a person who studies human history by digging sites and studying the artifacts and remains found in them

ARTIFACT
something made by a human, usually long ago

ATOM
the smallest unit of matter

BIOLOGICAL
relating to living things

CAVITY
an unfilled space within a mass

CHEMICAL
relating to the way substances interact with one another

CHEMISTRY
the area of science that studies how things are made and how different substances react when combined

CLIMATE
weather conditions in a certain area over a long period of time

COMPOSITION
how or of what something is made

CONGLOMERATE
a coarse sedimentary rock containing fragments of different materials

CRYSTALLOGRAPHER
someone who studies crystals in minerals and are experts in many areas of science

DECOMPOSE
break down, decay, or rot

ELEMENT
a substance found in nature that is in its simplest form

EROSION
the process in which wind, water, and ice wear away rock over time

EXTRUSIVE
forming on Earth's surface

FLUORESCENCE
absorbing light of one color and reflecting another, giving it the appearance of glowing

FOSSIL
the remains or imprint of an ancient animal preserved in part or whole in a sedimentary rock layer

GEMOLOGIST
someone who studies precious stones

GEODE
a crystal-filled cavity, or hole, inside a rock

GEOLOGIST
an expert in the study of Earth's makeup and physical history

IGNEOUS
rock formed from cooled magma or lava

INORGANIC
not coming from living things

INTRUSIVE
forming within the earth

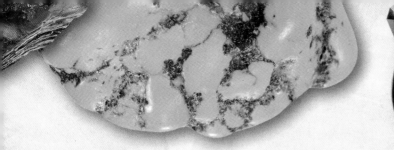

IRIDESCENCE
the ability to appear to glow or change colors when viewed from different angles

LUNAR
from the Moon

MAGMA
hot liquid found beneath Earth's crust

MAGNETORECEPTION
the ability to find direction using Earth's magnetic field

MARINE
of or in the sea

METAMORPHIC
rock formed by heat and pressure from sedimentary or igneous rock

MINERAL
a hard material from which rocks and gems are made that is found in nature and is not made of living things

MINERALOGIST
an expert in the composition, structure, and the properties of minerals

MOLTEN
rock that has been made into liquid by extreme heat

OPAQUE
not allowing light to travel through it; not transparent

ORGANIC
coming from living things

PALEONTOLOGIST
a scientist who studies fossilized plants and animals

POROUS
full of holes through which water or air can pass

RADIOACTIVE
releasing or containing radiation

RESIN
a sticky substance produced by trees and some plants

SEDIMENTARY
made from sediment deposited by wind or water

STRATA
rock layers in the ground

THEORY
an idea that tries to explain something

TOXIC
poisonous

UNIFORM
the same throughout

VOLCANO
a mountain or hill from which hot gas or vapor, rocks, and lava erupt from within the earth

WEATHERING
the different ways a rock is broken down at or near the surface

Tangerine Press®
an imprint of
■ SCHOLASTIC
scholastic.com

10 9 8 7 6 5 4 3 2 1

ISBN: 978-1-338-60337-8

Printed in Guangzhou, China
5009769   06/20

Scholastic Inc.
557 Broadway
New York, NY 10012

Scholastic UK Ltd.
Euston House
24 Eversholt Street
London NW1 1DB

Scholastic LTD
Unit 89E, Lagan Road
Dublin Industrial Estate
Glasnevin, Dublin 11

Photos ©: 2 main: Yuri_Arcurs/Getty Images; 4 atomic symbol: bubaone/Getty Images; 5 top right: Ekaterina Fribus/Dreamstime; 6 top right: greenphotoKK/Getty Images; 7 diamonds: BamBamImages/Getty Images; 9 coltan: John Cancalosi/Alamy Stock Photo; 9 magnitite: Goldminer/Dreamstime; 11 mica: okanmetin/Getty Images; 11 banana: kutaytanir/Getty Images; 12: Courtesy I. Huskić, I. V. Pekov, S. V. Krivovichev, T. Friščić Research Group/ McGill University; 13 top right: CARSTEN PETER/SPELEORESEARCH & FILMS/National Geographic Creative; 15 main: Dorling Kindersley/Getty Images; 15 bottom right: Justin Reznick/Getty Images; 21 red marble: aregfly/Alamy Stock Photo; 23 puddingstone: John Cancalosi/Alamy Stock Photo; 23 background: LWM/NASA/LANDSAT/Alamy Stock Photo; 25 bottom right: Al Freni/Getty Images; 26: Lee Ramey Ogle; 27 top right: courtesy Fossil Safari; 30 top: Universal Images Group North America LLC/Alamy Stock Photo; 30 bottom: Roman Sigaev/Alamy Stock Photo; 31 left: The Natural History Museum/Alamy Stock Photo; 31 bottom right: NASA; 33 bottom right: Courtesy D.NEA Diamonds; 34 top right: Royal Collection via AAP; 34 center: Royal Collection Trust/© Her Majesty Queen Elizabeth II 2020; 34 bottom right: AMNH/C. Chesek; 38 bottom right: sasacvetkovic33/Getty Images; 39 main: Georgy Shafeev/Science Source; 41 top left: Björn Wylezich/Alamy Stock Photo; 41 top center right: Björn Wylezich/Alamy Stock Photo; 41 top right: The Natural History Museum/Alamy Stock Photo; 41 bottom right: Jeffrey Isaac Greenberg 6/Alamy Stock Photo; 42: Courtesy Crystal Caves in Atherton, North Queensland, Australia; 43 left: Courtesy of A. Telfer/ Smithsonian Institution; 43 bottom right: Courtesy Utah Outdoor Activities; 43 top right: Roman Pats/Dreamstime; 44 mineralogist: SrdjanPav/Getty Images; 45 top left: Cultura Creative (RF)/Alamy Stock Photo; 47 center right: Ekaterina Fribus/ Dreamstime.

All other photos © Shutterstock.com.